The Month Of: 1 2 3 4 5 6 7 8 9 10 11 12

SUNDAY	MONDAY	TUESDAY	WEDNESDAY
○	○	○	○
○	○	○	○
○	○	○	○
○	○	○	○
○	○	○	○

THURSDAY	FRIDAY	SATURDAY	NOTES
○	○	○	
○	○	○	
○	○	○	
○	○	○	
○	○	○	

The Week Of: /   /

MONDAY

TUESDAY

THURSDAY

FRIDAY

WEDNESDAY	GOALS OF THE WEEK

SATURDAY/SUNDAY	NOTES

The Week Of: /   /

MONDAY

TUESDAY

THURSDAY

FRIDAY

WEDNESDAY	GOALS OF THE WEEK
SATURDAY/SUNDAY	NOTES

The Week Of: /   /

MONDAY

TUESDAY

THURSDAY

FRIDAY

WEDNESDAY	**GOALS OF THE WEEK**
SATURDAY/SUNDAY	**NOTES**

The Week Of: /   /

MONDAY	TUESDAY

THURSDAY	FRIDAY

WEDNESDAY	GOALS OF THE WEEK
SATURDAY/SUNDAY	NOTES

The Week Of: /   /

MONDAY

TUESDAY

THURSDAY

FRIDAY

WEDNESDAY	GOALS OF THE WEEK
SATURDAY/SUNDAY	NOTES

The Month Of: 1 2 3 4 5 6 7 8 9 10 11 12

SUNDAY	MONDAY	TUESDAY	WEDNESDAY
○	○	○	○
○	○	○	○
○	○	○	○
○	○	○	○
○	○	○	○

THURSDAY	FRIDAY	SATURDAY	NOTES
○	○	○	
○	○	○	
○	○	○	
○	○	○	
○	○	○	

The Week Of: /   /

MONDAY	TUESDAY

THURSDAY	FRIDAY

WEDNESDAY

GOALS OF THE WEEK

SATURDAY/SUNDAY

NOTES

The Week Of: /   /

MONDAY	TUESDAY

THURSDAY	FRIDAY

WEDNESDAY	**GOALS OF THE WEEK**
SATURDAY/SUNDAY	**NOTES**

The Week Of: /   /

MONDAY	TUESDAY

THURSDAY	FRIDAY

WEDNESDAY	**GOALS OF THE WEEK**
SATURDAY/SUNDAY	**NOTES**

The Week Of: /   /

MONDAY	TUESDAY
THURSDAY	FRIDAY

WEDNESDAY

GOALS OF THE WEEK

SATURDAY/SUNDAY

NOTES

The Week Of: /   /

MONDAY	TUESDAY
THURSDAY	FRIDAY

WEDNESDAY	GOALS OF THE WEEK

SATURDAY/SUNDAY	NOTES

The Month Of: 1 2 3 4 5 6 7 8 9 10 11 12

SUNDAY	MONDAY	TUESDAY	WEDNESDAY
○	○	○	○
○	○	○	○
○	○	○	○
○	○	○	○
○	○	○	○

THURSDAY	FRIDAY	SATURDAY	NOTES
○	○	○	
○	○	○	
○	○	○	
○	○	○	
○	○	○	

The Week Of: /   /

MONDAY	TUESDAY

THURSDAY	FRIDAY

WEDNESDAY

GOALS OF THE WEEK

SATURDAY/SUNDAY

NOTES

The Week Of: /   /

MONDAY	TUESDAY

THURSDAY	FRIDAY

WEDNESDAY	GOALS OF THE WEEK
SATURDAY/SUNDAY	NOTES

The Week Of: /   /

MONDAY

TUESDAY

THURSDAY

FRIDAY

WEDNESDAY	GOALS OF THE WEEK

SATURDAY/SUNDAY	NOTES

The Week Of: /   /

MONDAY | TUESDAY

THURSDAY | FRIDAY

WEDNESDAY	GOALS OF THE WEEK
SATURDAY/SUNDAY	NOTES

The Week Of: /   /

MONDAY	TUESDAY
THURSDAY	FRIDAY

WEDNESDAY	**GOALS OF THE WEEK**
SATURDAY/SUNDAY	**NOTES**

The Month Of: 1 2 3 4 5 6 7 8 9 10 11 12

SUNDAY	MONDAY	TUESDAY	WEDNESDAY
○	○	○	○
○	○	○	○
○	○	○	○
○	○	○	○
○	○	○	○

THURSDAY	FRIDAY	SATURDAY	NOTES
○	○	○	
○	○	○	
○	○	○	
○	○	○	
○	○	○	

The Week Of: /   /

MONDAY

TUESDAY

THURSDAY

FRIDAY

WEDNESDAY	GOALS OF THE WEEK

SATURDAY/SUNDAY	NOTES

The Week Of: /   /

MONDAY	TUESDAY

THURSDAY	FRIDAY

WEDNESDAY	GOALS OF THE WEEK
SATURDAY/SUNDAY	NOTES

The Week Of: /   /

| MONDAY | TUESDAY |

| THURSDAY | FRIDAY |

WEDNESDAY	**GOALS OF THE WEEK**
SATURDAY/SUNDAY	**NOTES**

The Week Of: ___ / ___ / ___

MONDAY

TUESDAY

THURSDAY

FRIDAY

WEDNESDAY	GOALS OF THE WEEK

SATURDAY/SUNDAY	NOTES

The Week Of: /   /

MONDAY	TUESDAY

THURSDAY	FRIDAY

WEDNESDAY	GOALS OF THE WEEK
SATURDAY/SUNDAY	NOTES

The Month Of: 1 2 3 4 5 6 7 8 9 10 11 12

SUNDAY	MONDAY	TUESDAY	WEDNESDAY
○	○	○	○
○	○	○	○
○	○	○	○
○	○	○	○
○	○	○	○

THURSDAY	FRIDAY	SATURDAY	NOTES
○	○	○	
○	○	○	
○	○	○	
○	○	○	
○	○	○	

The Week Of: /   /

MONDAY	TUESDAY

THURSDAY	FRIDAY

WEDNESDAY	GOALS OF THE WEEK

SATURDAY/SUNDAY	NOTES

The Week Of: __ / __ / __

MONDAY	TUESDAY

THURSDAY	FRIDAY

WEDNESDAY	GOALS OF THE WEEK

SATURDAY/SUNDAY	NOTES

The Week Of: /   /

MONDAY	TUESDAY

THURSDAY	FRIDAY

WEDNESDAY	GOALS OF THE WEEK
SATURDAY/SUNDAY	NOTES

The Week Of: /   /

MONDAY	TUESDAY

THURSDAY	FRIDAY

WEDNESDAY	GOALS OF THE WEEK
SATURDAY/SUNDAY	NOTES

The Week Of: /   /

MONDAY	TUESDAY

THURSDAY	FRIDAY

WEDNESDAY

GOALS OF THE WEEK

SATURDAY/SUNDAY

NOTES

The Month Of: 1 2 3 4 5 6 7 8 9 10 11 12

SUNDAY	MONDAY	TUESDAY	WEDNESDAY
○	○	○	○
○	○	○	○
○	○	○	○
○	○	○	○
○	○	○	○

THURSDAY	FRIDAY	SATURDAY	NOTES
○	○	○	
○	○	○	
○	○	○	
○	○	○	
○	○	○	

The Week Of: /   /

MONDAY	TUESDAY

THURSDAY	FRIDAY

WEDNESDAY

GOALS OF THE WEEK

SATURDAY/SUNDAY

NOTES

The Week Of: /   /

MONDAY	TUESDAY

THURSDAY	FRIDAY

WEDNESDAY	GOALS OF THE WEEK

SATURDAY/SUNDAY	NOTES

The Week Of: /   /

MONDAY	TUESDAY

THURSDAY	FRIDAY

WEDNESDAY	GOALS OF THE WEEK
SATURDAY/SUNDAY	NOTES

The Week Of: /   /

MONDAY	TUESDAY

THURSDAY	FRIDAY

WEDNESDAY	GOALS OF THE WEEK

SATURDAY/SUNDAY	NOTES

The Week Of: /   /

MONDAY	TUESDAY

THURSDAY	FRIDAY

WEDNESDAY	GOALS OF THE WEEK

SATURDAY/SUNDAY	NOTES

The Potato Eaters

LIST & THINGS TO REMEMBER

LIST & THINGS TO REMEMBER

LIST & THINGS TO REMEMBER

LIST & THINGS TO REMEMBER

LIST & THINGS TO REMEMBER

LIST & THINGS TO REMEMBER

LIST & THINGS TO REMEMBER

LIST & THINGS TO REMEMBER

LIST & THINGS TO REMEMBER

LIST & THINGS TO REMEMBER

Cafe Terrace at Night